Is Trump, Clintons Puppet?

By Simon Luria

Copyright information

Luria, Simon

Is Trump, Clintons Puppet?

—1st ed

Printed in the United States of America

Cover images : rudall30

(Rudolf Petrus Iskandar)

Book Cover Design: Simon Luria

Introduction

What you are about to read is an opinion piece, one that is not necessarily uniquely my own, but one that is shared by a growing number of people. Writing this book is risky, The Trump people and maybe even the Hillary people will demand that Amazon take it down. Why?

If you have been watching the election cycle on the news here in the United States you will know that Donald Trump is turning everything upside down. This is not necessarily a bad thing, our political system needs a jolt, but I was wondering if there was not something more going on here. Something seems wrong. Is Trump serious about becoming president? Or is he trying to destroy the Republican Party on behalf of the democrats?

In more blunt terms, is Donald Trump paving the way for Hillary Clinton's presidency? In this book, I will outline a few pieces of evidence that I think point exactly in that direction. Conspiracy theory you say? We shall see!

The Donald

You must admit, Donald Trump is a compelling person. He is the person you just love to hate. Despite that, he is incredibly effective at what he does.

Donald Trump was born on June 14, 1946, he used to be mostly known for his Real Estate development in NYC but he has since become a television personality, a role he seems most suited for. He was born into a rich family. His Father Fred was a major Real Estate developer in NY. Donald was slated to continue his father's legacy. In fact, he expanded his father's empire into Manhattan Real Estate at a time when prices were relatively depressed. The NY of that time was a cease pool of crime, but Donald had a vision. At first he did very well and was even listed in Forbes magazine among the world's Billionaires.

He became restless and decided to branch out into gambling. He opened several high profile casinos in Atlantic City, New Jersey. Those turned out to be very bad investments. As a result of many bad business moves, a few of the businesses had to go bankrupt, not once but several times. So much for his business prowess.

Business failings aside, he is mostly known now as a TV personality. His smash hit show the Apprentice kept him in the limelight. Being the restless man that he is, he decided to run for president of the United States, something most pundits called a short-lived stunt. Well, it was not as short-lived as they thought. As unlikely a candidate as he may be, he has since rocked the political establishment in ways that were completely unforeseen. All the stuffed shirt wonks and pundits got their panties in a bunch at the fact that he was able to get away with as much as he has. His political longevity is of utmost concern but many are starting to think, aside from his desire for being in the limelight, there is another reason he is running. We will discuss that in a future chapter. In the next chapter, we will discuss his various forays into politics. After that, we will discuss his possible intentions for running. I am convinced you too will see that perhaps Trump is really not running for president after all, but paving the way for someone else. That someone else, is Hillary Clinton. Conspiracy theory you say? We will get deeper into it later in the book.

Donald Trump's Frenetic Politics

Unlike most people who stay the same political affiliation all their lives or at the most change it once. Donald Trump has changed his several times.

In 1987, Donald Trump registered as a republican in NYC. This was in vogue amongst business leaders. Ronald Reagan was half way through his second term as President of the United States and most business people voted for him. In October of 1999 he switched affiliation and registered for the Independence party. In 2001 he decided that the independence party wasn't good enough and registered as democrat which lasted a good 8 years. He then switched parties once again and went back to the Republican Party, but that lasted all but 2 years. In 2011 he did not enroll in any party. In April of 2012, he returned to the Republican Party and has been there ever since.

His affiliation changes aren't based on moral grounds but mostly on business ones. As we discussed earlier Donald built a few casinos in Atlantic City. From 1996 to 2007 he made at least 12 contributions to the Republican Representative of the Second Congressional District in New Jersey, Frank LoBiondo. That is just one example of many.

His Donation records run the gamut. He has given heavily to both parties overall. One often needs to ask what the motives were each time. More importantly, what are his motives now? He has been a democrat most of his political life. Is he still one? Is he a false flag? A shill for Clinton? I say yes, but before we get deeper into that let us briefly explore Donald Trump's relationship to the Clintons.

Trump and the Clintons

It is public knowledge by now that the Clintons were at Donald Trump's 3rd wedding. Not only that, the Clintons were honored with a FRONT ROW SEAT to the event. It is also public knowledge that Donald contributed to the Clinton Foundation, the very foundation he is railing against now.

Not many know, although it too is public knowledge that Donald Trump and Bill Clinton have been friends for a very long time. And as a side note, Chelsea Clinton, Bill and Hillary's daughter is good friends with Trumps Daughter Ivanka. There is, of course, nothing wrong with that.

Bill Clinton even admitted that Trump has been, and I quote, "Uncommonly Nice to Hillary and Me." In an interview on CNN in 2012, Bill Clinton said "I like Him. And I love playing Golf with him." All this despite the fact that Trump was lampooning Barack Obama on the legitimacy of his presidency. Trump too has some very nice words to say about Clinton. He stated on Fox News that same year that Bill "…was a really good guy."

A few years prior to that, Donald came to Bills defense regarding the whole Monica Lewinsky Scandal he said "Look at the trouble Bill Clinton got into with something that was totally unimportant, and they tried to impeach him, which was nonsense,"—CNN Interview 9/2008. This seems to contradict his December 2015 tweet "If Hillary thinks she can unleash her husband, with his terrible record of women abuse, while playing the women's card on me, she's wrong!"

He appears to be contradicting himself. In one breath he claimed that Clinton was victimized but now he has outright said that he thinks Bill Clinton is a victimizer.

One can say their relationship changed when he became the Republican Candidate for president in direct opposition to Hillary. I understand that the gloves come off during presidential season. But that is not the case, it appears they remain friends.

The Washington Post reported that Trump and Bill Clinton had a private conversation in MAY of 2015 in which **Clinton encouraged Trump to Run for President under the republican ticket. This coming a month after Hillary announced her candidacy and a few weeks before Trump announced his own**. Later that month Trump bad mouthed Bill by calling him a rapist, THE **SAME MONTH AS THEIR MEETING**. It seems like they planned for Trump to run and "pretend" to be against the Clintons. Trumps sudden about-face is suspicious.

Something doesn't add up here. Let's revisit this again. Trump has a meeting with Bill Clinton, Clinton encourages Trump to run against his own wife. Trump suddenly announces that he is running for president and goes on to insult the very person he met with just 2 weeks prior? That is VERY suspicious. Don't you agree? Something is going on here.

Are Rumors Just Unconfirmed Facts?

That meeting I spoke of in the prior chapter is suspicious. Another thing I find odd is Donald Trump's response or lack of one to Hillary's most recent health scare.

If you have been watching him as of late, he has been questioning Hillary's health. In fact, he started his inquiry into her health in December of 2015. Here are a few examples of his statement son her health.

In Davenport Iowa he states **"She'll do a couple of minutes in Iowa, meaning a short period of time. And then she goes home. You don't see her for five or six days. She goes home, goes to sleep. I'm telling you. She doesn't have the strength. She doesn't have the stamina."**

That Same month he mentioned in "Meet The Press" **"I think that my words represent toughness and strength. Hillary's not strong. Hillary's weak, frankly. She's got no stamina; she's got nothing. She couldn't even get back on the stage last night."**

On ABC's "This week" He stated, **"Hillary is a person who doesn't have the strength or the stamina, in my opinion, to be president. She doesn't have strength or stamina. She's not a strong enough person to be president."**

On September 6th, 2016 Trump continued to discuss Hillary's health in response to a speech she gave in which she was experiencing a coughing fit. He tweets **"Mainstream media never covered Hillary's massive "hacking" or coughing attack, yet it is #1 trending. Whats up?"**

Trumps surrogates have also pointed out several videos that have been circulating that have been used to "prove" that Clinton is ill and unfit to be president.

Most know that previous claims of her being ill were simply conspiracy theories, there was no evidence that she had any illness whatsoever. Trump knew it and it's for this reason he felt safe harping on her health. However, something changed.

At a 9/11 memorial, Clinton was feeling ill, she had to leave early. She claimed she was "overheated". A few moments later she is stumbling into her car, it appears that she fainted.

Oddly enough, when Trump was asked about it, he states "I don't know anything about it". http://www.msnbc.com/msnbc-news/watch/trump-on-clinton-s-health-incident-762655811856

I can understand if he didn't want to detract from the 9-11 memorial activities which was nice of him. But a few days later he tweets"@realDonaldTrump **on Hillary's health: I hope she gets well, gets back on the trail & we'll see her at the debate."**

Donald seems a little sheepish doesn't he? At every corner he would mention her ill health and physical inability to be president. He isn't pouncing on her this time, I think that's because this is a real health crisis not a made up one. His silence speaks volumes to their TRUE friendship. He isn't showing tact or self-control that's not his M.O, he isn't pouncing because this is real. If he truly believed her health was an impediment he would have said something or at least hinted. This would have proven him correct about her health all along, yet he says nothing. His silence is simply too suspicious.

So why would Trump Be A Shill for Clinton?

Throughout his candidacy, his own party members have suspected that Trump might very well be a plant for Clinton intended not just to assure Hillary wins, but to wreak havoc on the GOP. They suspect this of course due to that phone call I mentioned in the previous chapter. Some Democrats are now thinking perhaps this is true. Democratic Congresswoman Marcy Kaptur is the only one who on record admitted her suspicions.

She states **"There are some theories on the Internet that this is Bill Clinton's best political deal," says Marcy Kaptur, the veteran Democratic congresswoman from Ohio and the House's longest-serving female lawmaker, "that he and Donald are buddies, and they have a lot of similar friends in New York, and he has masterfully selected a friend who maybe by October will say, 'You know, this is very boring. And I'm going to get out.'"** - - National Review

In 2008, Trump Supported Hillary Clintons presidential campaign and gave her high praises. He stated that she is " Very Talented, very smart." He also supported democratic leadership stalwarts such as New York Senator Chuck Schumer, Current Senator of Nevada Harry Reid. He also supported, in the past the late Ted Kennedy and the now disgraced Former rep Anthony Weiner. But in reality, his money is not what is helping Hillary the most. What he is doing is giving Hillary fodder against himself and the GOP on purpose. Hillary has used many of Donald Trump's own words against his fellow republicans. She of course also uses his own words against himself, which is the whole plan. He is intentionally being controversial as to provide ammo to the other side. This is all a game. Even top Republican think so. Jeb Bush stated in a tweet "Maybe Donald negotiated a deal with his buddy @HillaryClinton," Jeb Bush tweeted. "Continuing this path will put her in the White House."

The conservative blogger Justin Raimondo wrote in July 2016 "Donald Trump is a false-flag candidate...It's all an act, one that benefits his good friend Hillary Clinton and the Democratic party that, until recently, counted the reality show star among its adherents. Indeed, Trump's pronouncements – **the open racism, the demagogic appeals, the faux-populist rhetoric – sound like something out of a Democratic political consultant's imagination, a caricature of conservatism as performed by a master actor**."

Another thing that is suspicious is the fact that his children Ivanka and Eric Trump couldn't vote for their father during the republican primary. Why? BECAUSE THEY WERE REGISTERED INDEPENDENTS. Most but not all the Trump Family are tried and true

Independents and democrats and they always have been. Ivanka and Eric failed to change their political affiliations in time. To me, that is suspicious. They are his biggest advocates and yet somehow they forgot to change their political affiliation. It's very fishy.

Even Trump himself has slipped up a few times indicating he may not even except the presidency if he won the election. New York Times reporters presented Trump with the hypothetical scenario of winning the presidency, only "to forgo the office as the ultimate walk-off winner," Mr. Trump responded with a smile: **"I'll let you know how I feel about it after it happens."**

"I'll let you know how I feel about it after it happens." Was he being cute? I am not so sure. I don't think he has any intention to be president . He has FAR too much to gain by not being president. He will be making a tremendous amount of money after he "loses." He already has the popularity, in fact now he has more fans than ever. He could possible create a Trump TV as Advertising executive and TV personality Donny Deutsch suggested he might do.

Entrepreneur and Dallas Mavericks owner Mark Cuban illustrated how profitable an election loss would be for Trump. In fact, he called it a "Dream Scenario." This dream scenario would involve him winning the vote but losing the electoral college. As Cuban states " All the glory. None of the work," Cuban goes on to say that a loss to Hillary would increase his net worth nearly 10 fold.

Cuban goes on to say "His brand would lose the negativity. He could do anything he wanted in business,"
(http://money.cnn.com/2016/07/21/news/mark-cuban-donald-trump/)

So even the top business people know that this is all a sham. His reward for helping Clintons will be to increase his own status and financial worth. It's absolutely genius yet sinister at the same time.

My Prediction

Trump is only a few percentage points above Clinton as of the time of this writing. Watch him now make serious blunders. Watch him do whatever it takes to lose support during this next few weeks leading up to the election . He doesn't want to win folks this isn't about him, this is about Hillary. He already has plenty of escape hatches ready for him to use.

1. He can use the fact that his financial situation is so complex that being president will take him away from tending to his business. So he can use his business as an out to save face.

2. His children, Ivanka and Donald Jr recently had very tough interviews in which they both ended the interviews abruptly. Donald Trump may want to "protect" his children from the media and thus step down for the good of his family. Take a look at the videos of the interviews.

    Ivanka, Interview:

    https://www.youtube.com/watch?v=nKxxlftcYyY

    Donald Jr Interview:

    http://www.rawstory.com/2016/09/watch-trump-jr-abruptly-ends-interview-after-local-tv-reporter-asks-about-shady-family-foundation/

3. He can use his own foundation as a way to jump ship. The Trump foundation is currently under investigation for shady dealings. He may use that as an excuse to end the campaign stating that the foundation " has become a distraction."

He has more than one way out right now and he will use either these reason or another. He will make himself look like a victim of the system that he says is against him. He won't just simply concede defeat. I would be surprised if he even makes it to the Debate on September 26. If he does, he will botch it so badly that Clinton will surely win the election.

Hillary will get elected and that will make history, Bubba will be back in the White House. As far the republicans, this election will leave them a heaping , smoldering ruin. They will be defeated, and embarrassed. They will walk away with their tail between their legs. And in the end, Trump walks away richer and more powerful than he has ever been.

It is by far the greatest con job in political history.

Recommended Reading

Donald Trump: Make America Great Again: Donald Trump on Primaries, Illegal Immigrants, Terrorism, Hillary Clinton, Ben Carson, and Jeb Bush

Trump Talk Presents: 10 of Donald Trump's Most Controversial Political Statements--Straight from "The Donald" Himself

Donald Trump: "Make America Great Again": Understand Trump's Mindset

See How They Run: Campaign Dreams, Election Schemes, and the Race to the White House

PolitiGuide 2016: A Simple and Neutral Summary of the Most Important Issues in the 2016 Presidential Election

Current and Upcoming Books by the Author

www.simonluria.com

Current:

The Panama Papers: The Largest Financial Scandal of Modern Times

The NSA Hack and its Implications

 Is Big Pharma Behind The Ban on Kratom?

Is Trump, Clinton's Puppet?

UPCOMING:

The Self Victimization of A People: How Judaism Fosters
Antisemitism

Outlaws of Islam: The Great Satan of the East

Krokodil Tears: The Drug That Could Destroy the World

The False Promise of Reward: How Society Promotes Addiction

Source Material

Opensecrets.org

Followthemoney.org

http://www.newsweek.com/history-donald-trump-bill-clinton-friendship-464360

http://www.nationalreview.com/article/436740/donald-trump-bill-clinton-plant-theory-marcy-kaptur-speculates

http://www.cnn.com/2016/09/12/politics/trump-campaign-clinton-health-response/index.html

http://thehill.com/opinion/brent-budowsky/250445-brent-budowsky-is-trump-a-clinton-plant

https://www.washingtonpost.com/news/morning-mix/wp/2015/12/09/jeb-bush-jokes-of-trump-clinton-conspiracy-theory-heres-a-look-at-the-evidence/

http://www.nationalreview.com/article/428222/democrats-best-weapon-trump-mona-charen
https://www.commentarymagazine.com/politics-ideas/campaigns-elections/trump-helps-faltering-hillary/

http://m.jpost.com/Blogs/A-College-Perspective/Friend-and-Foe-Donald-Trump-Is-Working-for-Hillary-Clinton-463810#article=6017ODE1MzJDNTZCM0MwN0I2MTEwMkMwRjlGNkRGNkY0OTk=

https://www.theguardian.com/us-news/2016/apr/11/donald-trump-ivanka-eric-miss-vote-deadline

http://www.politicususa.com/2016/07/20/donald-trump-doesnt-president-united-states-attention.html

http://www.theblaze.com/stories/2016/08/02/msnbcs-donny-deutsch-claims-donald-trump-does-not-want-to-win-he-does-not-want-to-govern/

http://m.csmonitor.com/USA/Politics/2016/0708/Would-Donald-Trump-quit-if-he-wins-the-election

http://variety.com/2016/biz/news/michael-moore-donald-trump-1201838851/

About The Author

Simon Luria is a writer, raised in London and now based out of New York City. Far from flying under the radar, his name is often enough to start heated debates. On the one side, his fans adore him, always with their eye on his next book. On the other side, there is a vocal group of people who loathe Simon. These people vehemently oppose everything that he says, protesting him at every turn.

For his part, Simon makes no effort to quell this distaste, never seeking out controversy but at the same time never taking any steps to avoid it either. He lets the chips fall where they may. He sees the modern world as unnecessarily sanitized and politically correct, Simon refuses to fold under pressure, sticking to his principles, always telling it like he sees it. He is known for delivering blunt, well-researched musings on finance, geopolitics, foreign policy, religion, medicine, and the state of the world. His opinions have caused him to shield his true identity. It's the only way for him to produce the work he does without fear.

www.simonluria.com

www.ingramcontent.com/pod-product-compliance
Lightning Source LLC
Chambersburg PA
CBHW070135290526
45789CB00005B/2260